walk write (repeat)

walk write (repeat)

Sonia Overall

Published in this first edition in 2021 by:

Triarchy Press
Axminster, UK

www.triarchypress.net

ISBNs
Print: 978-1-913743-18-5
ePub: 978-1-913743-19-2
PDF: 978-1-913743-20-8

Illustrations by James Frost, Sonia Overall and Katy Whitaker

tp

Acknowledgments

Many thanks to all of the walkers and writers who have helped to road test these exercises.

Particular thanks to Andrew Carey, Phil Smith and Elspeth (Billie) Penfold for their interest and encouragement; to Katy Whitaker for her Distance Drift posters; to the many sync walkers on Twitter and in the Women Who Walk Network who have accompanied me on the way; and to James and Rowan Frost for their ongoing tolerance of my wanderings.

Contents

How to use this book

Walking and creativity

Walking helps you think. This has long been understood. Aristotle and his peripatetic philosophers walked about as an aid to thinking. The credo *Solvitur Ambulando* (it is solved by walking) is attributed to scholar and writer St Augustine. A scientific study carried out at Stanford University concluded that "walking increases creative ideation". Anyone who has ever taken a problem for a walk will know it to be true.

This book uses walking as a tool for creative thinking and writing. It is a manual for creative writers, but the approaches and exercises can readily be adapted by practitioners working in other media. All of the exercises included here have been foot-tested. Use the book to walk and work alone or in groups, together or separately. Use it to generate ideas, create text and read differently.

Walking outside, in varied environments, will offer you novel experiences to draw upon. Many of the exercises here can be carried out in your immediate environment, or if mobility or opportunity are an issue, in your own home. Rescale and adapt at will.

When using this book out walking, be respectful of others in public spaces, wear some suitable footwear and clothing, and please remember to take your common sense with you. Be open and playful. Enjoy the walk.

Section One

Creative walking: what and why

Creative thinking

As writers, we strive for originality of expression. Fresh, vital creative writing requires fresh, vital creative thinking: approaching things, however familiar, in a new way. So how do we go about thinking creatively?

There are various approaches that may be useful. We can hijack lateral-thinking puzzles, free association and brainstorming for wild ideas – those practices beloved by business gurus. These methods can kick-start ideas. Freewriting helps to switch on the creative brain: this is writing in the raw, without borders or theme or inner critic to interrupt, just the flow of words on a page. Freewriting can liberate language and help us to knock out new turns of phrase. Journaling gives us structure to support this. Reflective writing enables us to check-in with our intentions, focus our plans, consider our writing processes and learn what works, or doesn't, for our practice. Writing exercises that focus on using the senses and figurative description build on these foundations. But there will always be times when we draw a blank – when writing feels like churning the same old pot of words and ways. How do we refresh it? How do we look again and see something new?

I do it by walking. Walking as a creative writing method. Walking-writing: gathering materials, submitting to the sensory, exploring my home like a tourist, scouring the streets like a metal-detector in search of the hidden, the forgotten and the overlooked.

Embodied writing

Writers are thinkers. We spend a lot of time sitting at desks, spines compressing, legs numbing, carpal-tunnelling. We use our hands to write or type, our eyes to read and our minds to process. Aside from the odd moment of rehydrating or caffeinating, we can forget that we have bodies at all.

Without physicality in our writing, the world of our text will be nebulous. To be authentic, characters need to be bodies inhabiting real spaces, not floating bundles of motives and speeches. Objects need to be tangible. One way of ensuring this is to bring our bodies into our writing through movement and sensory experience.

Walking ticks those boxes. Walking and writing together – ambulatory writing – captures the process as it happens.

Inspiration

Inspiration also means 'to breathe in'. Walk. Get your lungs working. Go in search of ideas.

Psychogeography for writers

Psychogeography is the study of how different places affect our feelings, thoughts and behaviour. It's about noticing – and challenging – the passive way we often allow places and spaces to steer our behaviour. Think of psychogeography as a resistance movement: you will not blindly amble from A to B. Instead, you will notice and scrutinise A, B and everything in between.

Putting up some psychogeographical resistance will help you, as a writer, to sharpen up your observation skills. You will get to know, appreciate and continuously rethink your environment. You will begin to see 'real' and 'imagined' landscapes in the everyday. You will see stories in carparks and poems on street corners. Even your own living space will be a potential seedbed for propagating alien lifeforms.

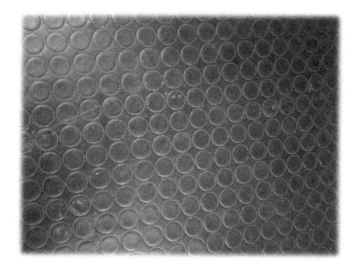

Creative walking: how

Methods

The Drift: Psychogeography uses the dérive or drift to explore place. This is a kind of walking that isn't about getting from one location to another, but about following your instinct and curiosity. There is no set destination in mind. There is only the will to be open to possibility.

The Catapult: A catapult is a prompt or intervention that speeds things up and gets you moving. This could be putting a dot on a map and finding your way there, flipping a coin to decide which way to go at a junction, or walking towards a distant landmark. Catapults can be used to start a drift, interrupt it or contain it.

Attentive walking: Drift, but with heightened awareness. You are seeking explanations – multiple explanations – for everything you encounter. Be open to the sensory, the physiological, the psychological and the aesthetic. Consider boundaries and planes, surfaces and edges.

Attitudinal walking: Walk attentively, but with a goal in mind or a lens to experience through. Walk with an attitude, idea or a problem. Walk to fix, solve or find. Walk in or as character, story or idea.

Totemic walking: Walk carrying an object in order to understand it more fully. The object can be a prompt for a new piece of writing, one that appears in a work in progress, or something more abstract or emblematic relating to a theme or idea you wish to explore.

Means

Carry a notebook. Get a pocket-sized one that opens, and stays open, easily. You might want one with a hardback cover for ease of pressure when writing. Take a camera or phone to capture images of intriguing objects, incidents or places that you want to come back to. If you find it difficult to write on the hoof, consider using a dictaphone or voice recording app and speak your ambulant thoughts.

If you have a map of your walking area, consider different ways of using it. Photocopy or trace a map so that you can overwrite, draw or write on, colour in or otherwise rework it. To walk the same space in different ways, draw figures on your map – from simple squares or crosses to complex designs – and use the lines as walking routes, following them as closely as you can. Or use your map to mark sites when you pause, or note moments of particular interest, creating a dot-to-dot record of your walk.

Write as you walk. Pause to make responsive and reflective notes as you need to. Write in stationary in-betweens. Generate a recorded stream-of-consciousness.

Take your time to explore and notice details. Stop and look, listen, touch surfaces, breathe in. Peer behind objects and street furniture. Look up above eye-level, down at knee-height and underfoot, ahead, aside and behind.

Aim for deep observations; keep detailed records. Try recording sensory experiences in different ways. **List as many attributes and characteristics** of a subject as you can. **List associations,** riffing on a word by recording synonyms or associated words to find new ways of describing a subject. **Label**, identifying flora and fauna. Use scientific, common or regional folk names – it doesn't matter which, but aim to be specific. If you do not know the name of a plant, or creature, or the purpose of a building or object, give it a name that makes sense to you. You can use figurative language to do this: don't be shy of employing metaphor or personification.

No walk is the same twice. Be prepared to repeat walks and exercises at different times and in different seasons. This enables you to note changes, however minute, in both the environment and in yourself.

Enter a dialectical mindset. The dialectic uses a back and-forth process of learning, framed as thesis (idea), antithesis (question) and synthesis (new knowledge). By questioning and testing as you walk, you will learn new ways of experiencing the world. You, the walker, are the thesis, carrying whatever ideas or intentions you may have. The environment you move through is the antithesis: the testbed for those ideas; the place for encountering opposites and obstacles; the field of experimental study. The walk itself is the synthesis, bringing both elements together to create new understanding. Once you have this synthesis, your writing is the means of articulating it. As the writer and theorist John Yorke points out in *Into the Woods*, the dialectic relationship is the basis of all stories, just as it is of all learning. As a writer, a curious observer, walk with 'what if?' uppermost in your mind. Ask questions and listen for answers.

Creative walking: ambulant writing exercises

The exercises in this section are divided into three types.

ℵ **Sparks**
Use a spark to get started on a walk or to switch things up during a longer walk.

∇ **Experiments**
Use an experiment to probe deeper.

↔ **Projects**
Use a project to develop a creative piece.

All exercises are designed to be carried out while walking. Get your notebook and pen (plus a spare) and start moving.

For catapults and prompts, see the DIY section.

א *Sparks*

א Six sensory sparks

1. SOUND. As you walk, **seek out interesting, strange and irritating sounds.** Write these down as you find them: try to transcribe sounds in different ways. Use onomatopoeic rendering to capture snippets of noise.

2. SOUND. Walk, **listening for contrasting sounds.** Write down all of the different sounds you can hear. Listen to the quietest and loudest, nearest and furthest. Walk further and listen for the shifts in volume and focus. How can you transcribe these different qualities?

3. SMELL. Seek out **different types of smells:** pleasing, nauseating, intriguing, familiar and unfamiliar. Record these smells using lists and labels.

4. SMELL. Walk until you **locate a single, distinct smell** to respond to, e.g. food stuff, object, perfume, plant. With this in sniffing distance, write about your smell. How can you describe a smell? Where does this smell take you? What memories or thoughts does it evoke? Walk with the smell permeating your thoughts, so that you move away from obvious connections. Smell, walk, write. Return to smell again, walk some more, write it down.

5. TOUCH. **Switch on your fingertips** and use them to explore your environment. Touch the ground beneath you, surfaces and objects. Walk in search of textures to explore. Carry the sensations with you as you walk; your fingertips will retain a trace of that last touch. How do the different textures feel? What emotions or associations do they evoke? Can you build a landscape of touch as you walk?

6. TOUCH. Find something that is **small enough to fit in your hand** and take it for a haptic walk. Feel its shape, weight and movement against your palm as you walk. Pause: hold it in your non-writing hand and write a description of the object as you *feel* it. Now hold the object with your eyes closed: tune into its shapes and textures. Open your eyes: describe the object as you *see* it. Walk with your object further to learn more about it.

ℵ Portals

Go through the nearest door, arch or gateway. Tune into the change of ambience as you step through the portal. What does this place hide or reveal?

How far can you travel using portals? How will you get back again?

ℵ Casting roles

Walk amongst other people.

Who can you see? Pick someone. Are they a hero or a villain? Are they an innocent bystander or a secret antagonist? What do they know that you don't?

How close dare you get to this individual? Do you need to flee before they spot you?

Write a quick character sketch to record your impressions.

Keep moving and encountering new characters in different settings.

ℵ Paranoia

Walk as if you are being followed. Listen out for footfalls behind you. Who looks suspicious? What was that noise? Walk faster. Keep looking back – there might be a story behind you.

א 3:1

You will need a timer for this algorithmic walk.

Set your timer for three minutes. Walk attentively and continuously. When the time is up, stop for one minute and record your impressions of the walk. Repeat at will.

This walk works best in a varied environment: if you need to traverse spaces that feel monotonous, extend the three minutes to six, taking longer walking stretches until the environment changes.

א Dystopia, utopia

Take an attitudinal walk in any environment. As you walk, apply a dystopian lens to your surroundings. Look for signs of decay and malaise. Record your impressions of walking in this desolate place.

Now apply a utopian lens to your walk: this is the best of all possible worlds. Look for evidence of beauty, growth and abundance. Record your impressions of walking in this place.

ℵ Dice roll

This walk embraces randomness and chance. You will need one or two dice and a timer.

Roll a pair of dice, or single die twice, and record the numbers. The first number gives you minutes, the second items. Set your timer for the number of minutes and start walking in search of items to fulfil the second number — objects, sites, buildings, creatures, plants — and record your impressions of them. If you have one minute and six items, you'll need to act fast: if you've got more minutes than items, take your time to select and describe.

Roll again to give you a new time and target, or repeat your original numbers as an algorithm.

ℵ Random settings

Take an attentive walk. As you go, find an unlikely setting for each of the following situations: i) an armed robbery ii) a marriage proposal iii) a political demonstration.

Write down a quick description of each setting. How might the situation subvert this place?

ℵ Other points of view

Take a short attentive walk in a pedestrian-friendly space: somewhere you won't bump into people or end up in a road.

Walk for a minute or so looking up. Pause to write a catalogue of everything you notice. Now walk looking down; pause to record.

Walk looking over one shoulder, then the other. Turn and walk backwards for as long as you can. Stop to record your impressions of experiencing this space in retreat and in reverse.

To flip perspective, try writing in the first-person voice of this space or items within it.

א Stuff and thingness

Take an attentive walk tuning into the tangibility of place. As you walk, pause to touch and sniff plants, walls and fences, manmade and natural objects. Treat each item as unique and specific. Knock and tap hard objects to test their percussiveness; gently squeeze and stretch soft or elastic items.

Write down descriptions of this 'stuff' using lists of words and associations. Test and consider shape, size, density, volume, weight, heft, tactility – not only the *thingness* of things, but also what writer James Wood calls the *thisness* of individual, material objects.

Walk and catalogue as you go.

▽ *Experiments*

▽ Soundshot

You will need a timer for this walk.

Set your timer for three minutes. Walk at speed until the timer rings. Stop and reset the timer for another three minutes.

Listen carefully to your surroundings. Explore the edges of these sounds by walking quietly around the immediate vicinity. Do not move beyond a few metres of your stopping place. You may want to close your eyes and tune in. When the timer rings, reset it for three minutes.

Now write down everything you can hear, however garbled or fragmentary: snatches of conversation, song lyrics, announcements, footstep sounds, birdsong, machinery noise etc. Record onomatopoeic renderings of sound (*cluk-cluk-cluk; fuuu-uugh; bleeeee*). Do not pause, reread or edit. When the timer rings, stop writing.

Repeat at will.

▽ Civil disobedience

Take an attitudinal walk in a busy place. Walk with an attitude of deference and politeness. Step aside for anyone coming towards you.

Balance this with a determination not to comply. Whenever you encounter directional signage, wilfully disobey or misread it. If an arrow points left, walk right. (Don't get run over.)

How does it feel to be bifurcated in this way? Try writing in this voice, showing both sides at once, inner and outer.

▽ Pathetic fallacy

Walk paying particular attention to the weather and quality of light. Let this become the lens through which you read the environment: if it is sunny and the blossom is out, the mood is optimistic and full of promise; if it is raining and getting dark, the mood is sombre and melancholic; wind is restless; and so on.

Make notes about the environment you pass through, applying this lens, either as a character (1st person) or on their behalf (external narrator). How can the details of place you observe be used to reflect mood?

Keep walking, writing your way into the mood as you go.

▽ Landmark

How far can you see? Look for the most distant landmark or furthest reach of your environment and describe this briefly. Walk attentively towards it, focusing on the visual.

Get as close to the landmark as is feasible in the time you have. Every few minutes, pause to describe the landmark again. Note how the experience of the landmark, and the way you perceive it, changes with increased proximity.

When you reach the landmark, explore it up-close, in forensic detail.

∇ Parameters, perimeters

Select a single, empty page of your notebook for this walk. Draw a cross diagonally through the page to divide it into four, like the back of an envelope.

Walk a defined perimeter: a square, a grid on a map, a block of streets, a circuit, a town wall, a fenced field... Do not stray from this border. As you walk along the first stretch, freewrite your thoughts (let them tumble out — no editing) into the top right-hand section of your page. Rotate your notebook as you go if it helps. Do not cross the lines.

When you get to the second stretch of your walk, move onto the top left-hand corner of your page; the bottom left-hand corner for the third stretch; and the final stretch in your remaining quarter.

How does it feel to be contained and constrained in this way? How does it affect your writing?

▽ Autoethnographic walk

Autoethnography is a study of oneself in relation to the world, considering the autobiographical in a wider context. Choose an object that is meaningful to you to carry on this walk. Ideally it should be comfortable to hold; if need be, carry it in a rucksack. An item of clothing or wearable object works well too.

Take a totemic walk with your object. Walk freely, giving the object your focus. Think through the memories and associations it has for you; record these as you walk. Stop to reconnect with your object (through sight, smell, touch) whenever your focus slips — if it is in a bag, keep taking it out to refresh those connections. Consider your object in relation to the different environments you walk through. Where does it belong? Where is it incongruous? Where did it come from and where has it been?

At the end of your walk, gather your notes together to write about the memories that your object evoked.

∇ Same space three ways

Take an attentive walk in an enclosed space, e.g. a public library, gallery, shopping centre etc. List details and sensory responses to the space: dimensions, colours, sounds, objects, light and shade, smells, temperature and so on.

Walk the space again, in character, as someone trapped here. Write as you walk, recording your impressions in your preferred point of view (1st, 2nd or 3rd person). Your character has never been here before, and they need to escape.

Walk the space again, in character, as someone who never wants to leave here. Write as you walk, recording your impressions using the same point of view. This is your character's home and they will stay whatever happens.

Reread your accounts. How have you used the same space to convey different situations and emotions? How were your characters affected by the space and the behaviour of those around them?

▽ Labyrinths and threads

Labyrinth walking lends itself to problem solving: a labyrinth is not a maze for getting lost in, but a single path that the walker must trust and follow. As the route is determined for you, all you need to do is walk and reflect.

There are numerous labyrinths in public spaces – find one if you can. If you have the time and space, construct a simple labyrinth for your own use (e.g. in a garden with string and pegs; on a sandy beach with a stick; on paving with chalk). You can draw a path to follow, or define 'walls' to contain the path. The website www.labyrinthos.net hosts designs of labyrinth types, instructions for creating your own labyrinth and links to labyrinth locators.

You can, however, turn any space – even a room in your home – into a site for labyrinth walking. Rather than imposing a labyrinth design on it, or constructing walls, let the space itself define the path. Identify the central point of your space and place an object there. Create your labyrinth path by walking circuitously towards that object. Imagine you are leaving a breadcrumb trail or unspooling a thread for others to follow. To begin with, walk the perimeter of the space, as tight to the edges as walls and furniture will allow. When you approach your starting point, turn 180 degrees, take a couple of steps towards the centre, and walk back on yourself. Keep repeating this, creating a path with curving 'ends' that loops around inside the space. When you get close to the centre, take a straight line to meet it. You have arrived at the centre of the labyrinth. Stay here a while, then walk out the way you came to unwind the thread.

For an even simpler version, walk a slow spiral towards the centre point.

For a large-scale labyrinth, draw your path on a map and follow it by walking.

Walk your labyrinth with a single 'nugget' in mind – a question, theme, word, idea, character – whatever is useful right now. When you get to the centre, make notes of your thoughts so far. Walk back out, considering further. Make reflective notes on your exit.

If you are unable to walk today, let your fingers follow the path of a drawn labyrinth (see DIY section).

▽ Walking line edits

i) **The hiatus.** Take an existing text that you want to edit on a walk. Use a labyrinth or meandering path to follow. Read the text to yourself as you walk (see Walking-Reading section; choose your space wisely). Whenever the path changes direction, stop and mark that point in the text. When you have finished the walk, use those marks to rework your text. Turn them into line breaks or end points for cut-ups. Make them peaks and troughs. Let the walk reshape predictable sentence constructions.

ii) **The stream.** Walk a meandering path or labyrinth. Freewrite as you walk, avoiding all punctuation. Stop when you get to the centre of the labyrinth or natural end to your path. Walk back again, reading the text to yourself. Use twists and coils in the path as moments to pause, punctuate and edit your text.

▽ Journey indoors

Walk your living space to reconnect with and defamiliarise it. Start at the threshold and walk systematically in and around each space. If you are working in a single room, divide the space into sections.

Walk your fingers along surfaces. Explore the textures of upholstery. Treat spots of light like islands to stand in, and try out all resting places. Consider objects in your home as artefacts in a museum of your life. What does each item represent? What do you cherish? What do you keep out of a sense of duty? What would you like to be rid of?

When you have fully explored a space, pick up an item – an object or small piece of furniture – and walk with it into the next space. Place the item there and explore as before. Repeat until you have scoured the whole of your living environment, relocating items to new territories.

↔ *Projects*

↔ Synchronicity

Take an extended attentive walk. Don't be led by landmarks: try to treat all buildings and obstacles equally. If you are in a busy place, walk against the current of the crowd.

Look for alternative directions to follow. Ignore road signs and arrows – look instead for any text or images that might lead you. Follow street names, advertisements, graffiti or shop signs that you can reinterpret as commands. Look for patterns, repeated numbers or groupings of objects: clusters of meaning.

Search for synchronicity. Can you find a thread running between the scenes, people or objects you encounter? Keep a record of directions, connections and coincidences.

Write up your walk. Is this a work of fragments or a fluid tale? What themes emerge? What images present themselves? What is the mood or tone?

↔ Sound narrative

Walk in an area with a flowing crowd (e.g. a high street). Listen in. What are people around you saying? Write down lines that reach your ears.

What connects these lines? Is there a conversation building? Is there a theme?

What environmental noises can you hear, or not hear (e.g. birdsong, water, sirens, music)? How does this relate to your recorded lines of speech? Pause and close your eyes if you need more focus.

Keep going. Let the sounds that are present (or absent) become your narrative focus. What is your walking environment trying to tell you? How is sound emanated or deflected from the structures that you pass? What do footfalls sound like here? Imagine that the ground beneath you is trying to tell you something: what is it? Can anyone else hear it, or is it only you? Decode and record the sound narrative of this place.

↔ **Three Act Quest**

Before you walk, select i) a protagonist, ii) a fantastical object, and iii) an obstacle. Make a note of these. Decide on the length of your walk and divide that time into thirds: these are your three walking Acts.

Act I: The Journey Out. Walk *as* your protagonist 'hero' in search of that object. Shed your everyday self and completely inhabit this protagonist persona. How do you feel about the environment you must traverse? What are you taking with you? Why do you need that object? What are you willing to do to get it?

Act II: The Destination. The object is close at hand, but first you must overcome your obstacle. Explore your immediate environment. Who or what is against you? How will you overcome it? What are you willing to do to get that object? Where is it to be found, and what is protecting it? What, if anything, can you call upon to help you?

Act III: The Journey Back. You have your object. Now you must get it safely home. Walk back to your starting point: how is the world different, now that you have achieved your goal? Do further obstacles present themselves? What have you learned on this quest?

↔ Contained behaviour

Walk in a contained public space (e.g. museum, shopping centre, market).

Record whatever snatches of speech you hear.

Note down the appearance and interactions of others. How does this space make people move and behave? How does it affect them? How does it affect you? What unspoken rules of behaviour apply here? Keep moving.

Choose two characters to work with, either from a work in progress or new creations (you could base them on people you have seen in this space). Give each character a line or two of overheard speech from your notes

Stop walking. Bring your characters together, using the spot you are standing in as their meeting place. Link their lines of speech to create a dialogue. Patch or tweak as required to make this work.

Get your characters to disagree. Stage an argument. Add facial expressions, body language and broader actions to convey anything that is not said directly. How will these characters behave in this contained space? How loud will they be? Will they hold it down, or will one or both of them break the rules of this space?

↔ **Secret street**

Walk in a residential area. Record your impressions of the buildings around you, the shape of the streets, any landmarks, parks, corner shops and so on. Look for details that are comfortable and familiar.

Stop when you come to a corner.

Now walk *as* character. You have just taken a habitual walk through your neighbourhood. The next street you see is completely alien to you: *it* has never been here before. Walk slowly, experiencing it for the first time, describing everything afresh. Scrutinise the facades of buildings. How did this place suddenly appear? Why was it hidden before? Why has it been revealed now? Can anyone else see it, or is it only you that has access?

Walk back, carrying the knowledge of this secret street with you. Write how you feel about it. Do you trust your own experience? What will you do with this extraordinary insight?

How might you explain it — as a parallel universe, a hallucination, a supernatural phenomenon...?

↔ Pan and zoom

Take the landmark walk (see Experiments) to the next level. Walk attentively towards a landmark, pausing to record your changing impressions as you draw closer. Aim for cinematic detail. As you walk, visualise your eye as a camera lens taking in a wide angle shot of the landscape, then a midshot of the landmark, then a close-up.

Write a description of this pan and zoom experience from the furthest distance to the closest detail.

Now place a character in shot. Who are they? Why are they heading towards this landmark? What will happen to them when they get there?

Use your walk back to think through and make notes about the unfolding narrative.

↔ Decreasing circles

If you have map of your walking area, draw a circle on it. This will contain your walk. Make the size of the circle according to the time you have available: walking this will take up roughly one third of your walking time. If you don't have a map, draw a circle in your notebook and make a note of your starting place: find a feature or landmark that is fixed, so you can return to it.

Walk the circle, gathering and recording details of your environment. When you return to the starting point, stop and read back through your notes. Circle five words or images that you find interesting.

Draw a smaller circle within the first and find a starting place on this circuit. Repeat the instructions above. When you return, circle three words or images.

Draw a dot at the centre of your circles and walk to it. Explore and record the immediate environment of your central point. Select one word or image from your notes for this section.

Write out your nine words or images. Walk back to your starting place, turning these over in your mind, seeking connections between them.

Write a short piece (vignette, poem, microfiction) using all of your selected words. What is at the heart of your piece – is it the central point, or the return? Use the words in whatever order works.

This walk can be extended using multiple decreasing circles and additional sets of words.

↔ Gulliver

Take an attitudinal walk. Walk *as* character: you are an explorer encountering new terrain.

Follow your curiosity. Wilfully misread signage, take advertisements literally, and note down any found text that strikes you as amusing, bizarre or ripe for misinterpretation.

What sights do you encounter? What are the locals like? Do you spot any unusual creatures (living, inanimate or imagined?) What do you stumble across? Give new names to your discoveries. Corrupt and readapt your found text: treat these snippets as literary artefacts or localised rules of behaviour.

Take sufficient notes as you walk to tell a fantastical version of your exploration on your return home.

↔ **Unnatural history**

Find an apparently innocuous municipal, institutional or historic building, stately home or other grand structure that you can walk around freely, inside or out.

Take an attitudinal walk looking for evidence of this building's hidden, guilty history. What clues do you find? Interrogate cornices and architectural frills for masonic signals. Look for messages in dropped litter, graffiti and fading signage. How do those working or visiting here behave? How much do they know?

Use your ambulant notes to sketch an alternative biography, historical fiction or unnatural history of the site. If your sketch has potential, use this building as a key setting for a longer piece of writing.

↔ **Retail haiku**

Walk in a shopping centre, supermarket or high street. As you walk, record descriptions of goods, sales displays and found text. Keep going until you have a couple of pages or more of text to work with.

Go through your notes and circle any words or phrases that you find interesting.

Choose a retail item or group of items from your descriptions. Find a way of simply describing, and then defamiliarising, the item(s). Look at your circled words – what can you use? Consider how playing with juxtaposition might create unusual phrases or imagery.

Use your text to create an imagist 'call and response', two-line haiku. Aim for a long first line and a shorter answering second line: Ezra Pound's poem 'In the Station at the Metro' uses a syllable pattern of 12/7. Try this:

i) call – write a single, descriptive line that presents your retail item

ii) response – write an answering line that defamiliarises or subverts the item, using figurative language or metaphor.

You may find that walking back and forth along a street or supermarket aisle helps you to get this bipedal striding, from one way of seeing to another, into your poem. Use the act of walking to bring rhythm to your lines. Use footfalls to count syllables, pace out the metre and test your line lengths.

If you prefer a traditional haiku format, use two lines for the 'call' and one for the 'response', creating three lines with a syllable pattern of 5/7/5.

Repeat at will.

Section Two

Walking-reading: what and why

Some people can walk and read at the same time. Walking and reading sounds like an idyllic way to pass the time, an ideal occupation for romantic heroines who don't mind a bit of grass-stain on their petticoats. Anna Burns' protagonist in *Milkman* is a walking reader; unfortunately, while this drifter's attention is diverted by *Ivanhoe*, she doesn't notice the very real dangers she is straying into.

If I read and walked at the same time, I would probably fall in a ditch. I would also feel like I was missing out on a vital element of walking: noticing my surroundings. Reading and pacing a study; reading and walking a treadmill or labyrinth; reading and ambling about the garden: this practice is safe enough and there is less to miss. Outside, a more provocative and creative approach is walking-reading, a process of walking yourself into a fictional landscape. Walking-reading offers an embodied way into understanding text.

Walking-reading can be achieved through attitudinal walking. The attitude to take on this walk is a text: a passage, a poem, a whole novel, an entire fictional world. We can apply attitudinal lenses to defamiliarise our environment, seeing it differently and responding to it creatively. This is what fiction does; walking-reading particularly lends itself to 'storying' spaces. As with writing, so with reading.

Walking-reading gives you, as a reader, fresh insights into the themes and settings of texts. As good writers must be good readers, this is another way to consider the potential reader experience of your own work.

Walking-reading: how

Methods

Apply the lens of your text and walk into that narrative world. Interpret your environment through its textual perspective. Draw parallels. You can start by thinking: 'that gate is intimidating'. From there it's a small step – simile to metaphor – to thinking: 'this is The Black Gate of Mordor' or 'beyond this lies Hill House'. As you settle into defamiliarising and reinterpreting your surroundings, those associations will become bolder. That burnt-out ruin is Manderley, Poynton or Thornfield Hall; that crumbling wall the perimeter of Carfax Abbey or the Castle of Otranto.

Walk *in* character, consciously adopting the role of protagonist, to access an embodied version of that character's part in the story. Walking in character is a bridge between your own experience in the landscape – here, now, in your own body – and the character's experience in their immediate world. You do not have to walk *as* character here; walking like them should suffice. You are seeking to interpret and understand them on your own terms, not to become them.

Walk *with* the characters of a fiction, experiencing the imagined landscape of a novel or series as if, like a first-person player in a video game, you have found yourself inside it. Immerse yourself. Write yourself into the fiction.

Bear witness to the world of the text at one remove. Consider your environment as if a scene in your chosen text were about to play out here. Or explore it as if the world of your text, or a pivotal moment in it, has already occurred, and you can detect the remnants of it. See that world through your eyes in the here and now.

Means

Be playful. Be imaginative. Walking-reading is a creative process: treat objects and structures as emblematic rather than worrying about literal representations.

Carry the text with you. Stop to read passages and revisit scenes. Read aloud to your environment. (Walk and read at the same time if you must.)

Narrate your way into the walk, internally or externally. Offer yourself a stream-of-consciousness articulation of the experience; make notes if it helps you to process what you see.

Walking-reading works well with others. Gather some fellow readers and explore together.

Read on for some walking-reading examples.

Walk Like Wells

Text: *The War of the Worlds*, H.G. Wells

Premise: Take a dystopian derive, seeking evidence of alien invasion.

Walk into the danger zone. Be vigilant. This threat can readily strike from above: look up for tripods, at the horizon for cylinders, and in the sky for flying machines.

Move as one evading detection. Beware surveillance equipment, reflective surfaces and glinting metal. Machines are the enemy. If you spot anything with three legs, run.

Keep away from the colour red: red weed signifies a site of Martian occupation. Look for safe, green, leafy areas to move through or rest unobserved. Stick to these where you can.

Holes in the ground are sites from which cylinder machines have emerged. Be cautious here. Toppled safety barriers are ineffective police cordons.

Bells and alarms warn of alien attack.

Towards the close of your walk, look for evidence of aftermath and repair: dereliction, scaffolding at scenes of destruction, and the slow return to normality after the aliens' defeat.

Wide Sargasso Walk

Text: *Wide Sargasso Sea*, Jean Rhys

Premise: Take a Gothic walk through this prequel to *Jane Eyre*, from the lush Caribbean to the ordered English countryside.

Look for evidence of *obeah*. There are signs of magic everywhere.

Beware *zombi* – anyone walking towards you could be possessed or soulless.

Walk with Antoinette (aka Bertha), looking for dense foliage and quiet leafy corners to hide in. Be wary of anything combustible: fire and smoke bring destruction.

Being indoors feels like a prison; avoid buildings, especially those with high windows. Get too close and you may walk into a trap.

Walk with Antoinette's unnamed husband (aka Rochester).
Go in fear of the wild and exotic. Seek symmetry, neat
spaces, trimmed lawns, borders and barriers. Celebrate
anything contained or hemmed in. Directional and
instructional signage is a welcome reminder of civilisation.
Towards the close of your walk, look for places that
juxtapose order and chaos.

Walking with Riddley

Text: *Riddley Walker*, Russell Hoban

Premise: Take a walk through the post-apocalyptic future in search of a lost civilisation, destroyed by atomic explosion.

Walk with Riddley, seeking remnants of a previous age: ruins on the landscape, objects in the ground, pits and holes signalling unearthed treasures. Circles are potent. Tread carefully

near these and keep your distance. Look out for rusted metal, broken machinery and humming pylons.

Beware all signs of industry, chemistry and dangerous technology. The secret of gunpowder production is kept by *chard coal berners*: keep away from smoke, alder trees, red sap and glimpses of red clothing. If you see any yellow stones, pick them up to keep them safely out of the hands of others.

Fences and gates indicate habitation. Look out for sharp poles or spikes for displaying heads. Beware dogs. Walk with a puppet in your pocket. Walk with feely stones in your hand. Practice your *Bad Luck go a way syn*.

Walk as an *Inlander* long after Riddley's time. Seek signs that the landscape has healed and civilisation is being restored. Look for clues that history might repeat itself, and how to prevent it.

Walk before the fall. What will survive the nuclear winter, and what will be lost?

Section Three

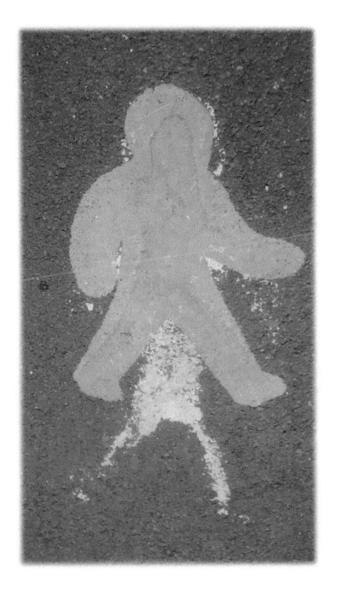

Creative walking-writing: DIY toolkit

Prompts, directions and instructions

The pages that follow are designed to be cut out, shuffled and carried while walking. Draw upon them when you need to shift gear on your walk.

Use the directions and instructions as **catapults** to help you drift, moving away from familiar routes. You could use a short series of these to create an algorithm for your walk.

Use the **writing prompts** to help you to see your immediate environment through a particular lens.

If you prefer your book intact, deploy an act of bibliomancy: flick through this section, close your eyes and point a finger at the page. Wherever it lands, you follow.

Or visit www.triarchypress.net/walkwritecutouts and print out the following pages so you can cut them up easily.

Catapults: directions

Walk straight for 100 steps.	Take the next right turn.	Take the next left turn.
Turn 180 degrees.	Walk on tiptoe for the count of 50.	Find an opening and look through it.
Find an arrow. Go the other way.	Cross to the other side.	Walk a figure eight.

Catapults: ways to walk

Look for mountains, literal and figurative.	Walk as quickly as you can.	Walk in a circle, looking for squares. Walk in a square, looking for circles.
Seek trinities: the number 3, trios and triangles.	Walk as slowly as you can.	Find a colour. Follow it.
Walk along a safe edge as if it is perilous.	Look for shields and force-fields.	Get away from here now!

Writing prompts (1/2)

Something is hidden here.	It came from the sky.	This is the last of its kind.
This is not what it seems.	You do not belong here.	A crime is taking place.
It came from the ground.	A ghost inhabits this.	This is holy Ground.

Writing prompts (2/2)

A game is being played.	An unexpected delivery is about to arrive.	A border begins here.
This is a nest.	A natural disaster is about to occur.	This is the HQ of a secret organization.
This is a screen.	Ley lines meet here.	This is a ticking bomb.

Creative walking-writing: Distance Drifts

Distance Drifts are suitable for walking indoors or out. Use the prompts to explore new spaces or freshen up the familiar.

Originally designed for individuals to share through a synchronised drift, walking alone together, these prompts are ideal for groups as well as lone creative walkers. Choose a drift, walk separately in sync, and share your responses. Suitably playful for family walks. For some example interactions, see #DistanceDrift on Twitter

SUNDAY, 28 JUNE, 10am - 11am (-ish)

follow @SoniaOverall #DistanceDrift for the instructions...

... tweet about what you see, hear, find...

...take care of your privacy and keep your distance !

JOIN IN A #DistanceDrift : at home, in your garden, or locality!

Join-the-dots

Walk by joining the dots. Find a dot of any size or colour in your immediate environment. Then another, and another. Keep going. Notice how your dot-spotting senses attune as you walk. Do any patterns emerge? Do any colours stand out? Where does joining the dots lead you?

Aquadrift

By a river or coast? Walk with this water, keeping it in sight and smell as much as you can. Landlocked or indoors? Walk like a diviner, sensing the presence of water out of sight. Seek out taps, drains, vessels, spouts, hoses, gutters and water signage.

Carry water to offer in libation (or consume) at favourite spots on your route. Make impromptu well-dressings to leave at water sources.

Widdershins

According to the OED, the etymology of 'widdershins' is other way, or against the sun.

Walk in the opposite direction you would normally take. Bear left. Take the left-hand path.

Explore spaces, objects and landmarks anticlockwise. Seek out opposites, inversions and contradictions.

Staying home? Walk your living spaces the same – opposite – way.

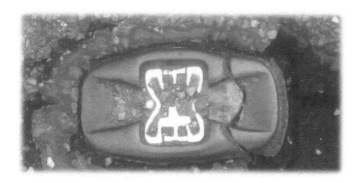

Monster walk

Walk on the trail of monsters: large or small, predatory or cute, lurking or lost. Look for the following clues:

1: Footprints; shed fur/scales/feathers/claws; paths of flight or trespass.

2: Evidence of feeding habits.

3: Anti-monster defence systems, established by others to repel or contain.

4: Habitation - dens, lairs or nests; temporary hiding spaces.

Scavenger Hunt

Go for a hands-free scavenger hunt, collecting items with your eyes. Write notes and take photos of your finds if you wish.

Find a (metaphorical) container to put your gathered items in. Size and weight is no object.

Find items in the following shapes: cone; ovoid, pyramid.

Find something black. Find something golden.

Find stripes, scrolls and interlinking patterns.

Find a bridge. Find something troll-like living beneath it.

Look down to find something buried. Look up to find something suspended.

Search for stars.

Pareidolia

Walk exploring pareidolia, the tendency to see patterns in the environment.

Look for faces on the furniture; in wood grain; in architecture.

Seek out animal shapes in pavement stains and the angles of street furniture. Detect the wings, jaws or bug-eyes of hidden insects in floral fabrics.

Search, like Hamlet, for the shifting shapes in clouds.

Mascot

Walk carrying a small fellow traveller in the form of a mascot: something that represents you and fits easily in one hand. Use a toy or mini-figure, or make something out of found objects, Lego or plasticine.

Your miniature haptic mascot serves three functions on this walk:

Your mascot will root your memory of this walk, serving as a hook between now and the future. See this mascot in a month or a year, and you will remember this walk.

It's fun. It's playful. A little silliness will help your creativity.

Your mascot is a miniature explorer, an extension of yourself.

Take it to places that you would like to go, but cannot reach or squeeze into. Put it on a shelf, under street furniture, in a hole in the ground – anywhere you cannot go physically, but might explore imaginatively.

Follow your curiosity – and your mascot's.

Islands

Walk looking for islands, indoors or out: islands of light and shadow; isolated features; an archipelago of moss patches on a wall.

Walk in search of bottled messages, seeking islands of found text. Which of these are you willing to uncork? How would you respond to such a message?

Seek out evidence of past shipwrecks and marooned survivors.

Decide where to pitch your survival tent – or your sun-lounger.

Bug walk

Walk adopting the attitudes and patterns of an insect on the go.

Ant: walk in straight lines; keep to single file; explore perimeters. Nothing is beyond your reach. Find something you'd like to carry home with your super-ant-strength, if you had it.

Butterfly: flit between points of interest. Look up! Pause and spread those wings.

Woodlouse: scuttle, seeking damp, shady places. Find something woody to chomp on and call home. Hide if you want to.

Bee: look for bright, colourful attractions and strong scents. Head straight towards them if you can. (Feel free to waggle dance.)

Ladybird: take a meandering, mazy path in search of something sweet.

End by walking as the next insect you encounter, or channel the creature of your choice.

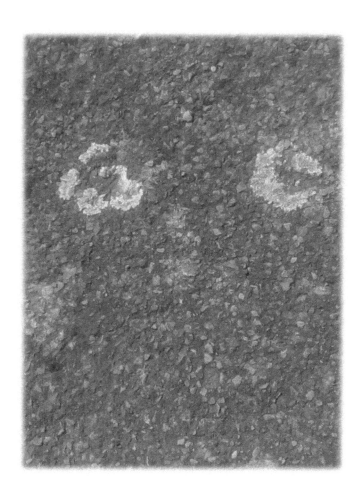

Time warp

Indulge in some low tech, pedestrian time travel.

Find a portal. Take a deep breath, hold on tight and step through.

You have transported fifty years into the past. How can you tell? Look for signs of the year you are now in.

Find a time machine. Let it take you to whenever you wish to visit. Repeat at will, seeking clues of the time you have travelled to.

To return to your present, find a time's arrow and follow it home.

Finger labyrinth for non-walking days

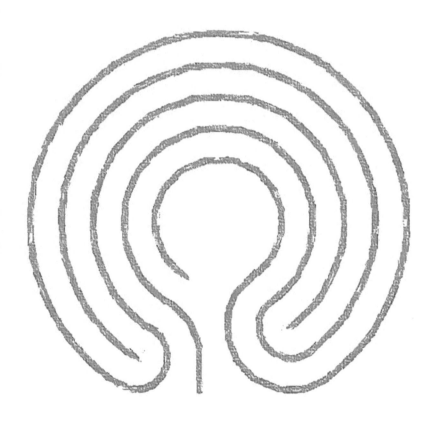

Space for notes

Further reading

There are numerous books that make creative use of walking, consider the history of walking and present walking protagonists. Here are a few suggestions to get you started: look around and you will find plenty more.

Psychogeography. Guy Debord's seminal essay 'The Theory of the Derive' was published in 1959 and can easily be found online. Merlin Coverley's acerbic potted history *Psychogeography* gives a useful historical overview of the main movements. *Walking Inside Out*, edited by Tina Richardson, offers more diverse voices in 21st Century British Psychogeography, including much under-represented women psychogeographers.

Walking and text. Iain Sinclair is a frequent figure in this landscape. Walking with a literary lens appears most accessibly in his book *London Orbital*, especially when he walks with *Dracula*. Phil Smith's post-apocalyptic guide *A Footbook of Zombie Walking* takes the zombie mythos as its lens and includes instructions for walkers.

Walking and writing. Merlin Coverley again: his *The Art of Wandering* discusses canonical walking writers. Lauren Elkin's book *Flâneuse* considers women walkers in the city, with sections on walking writers Jean Rhys and

Virginia Woolf. Browse numerous titles by Phil Smith (aka Crab Man), including fiction and poetry, to explore Mythogeography, his playful adaptation of psychogeographical approaches.

Contained walking. Xavier de Maistre's 18th-century travel satire *A Journey Around My Room* demonstrates the narrative potential of the smallest spaces. Clare Qualmann and Claire Hind's *Ways to Wander the Gallery* offers provocations for engaging with public exhibition spaces. For more on labyrinth walking, see Jeff and Kimberly Saward's generous online resource www.labyrinthos.net.

The science. If at the end of this journey you need scientific justification for walking (or you need to prove it to a disbeliever), the Stanford study by Marily Oppezzo and Daniel L. Schwartz, 'Give your ideas some legs: The positive effect of walking on creative thinking', was published in the *Journal of Experimental Psychology* in 2014. Numerous extracts and reviews of the findings exist online. Quote it whenever you need to excuse yourself to take a stroll.

About the Author

Sonia Overall

Dr Sonia Overall is a writer, psychogeographer and Senior Lecturer in Creative Writing. She creates prose, poetry and text for performance, and experiments with things that fall through the gaps in between.

Sonia is the founder of the 'Women Who Walk' network of walking artists and academics. She often leads playful, performative and interactive walks, workshops and walkshops, and can be found in residence at festivals and public spaces.

www.soniaoverall.net
@soniaoverall

About the Publisher

Triarchy Press is a small, independent publisher of books that bring a wider, systemic or contextual approach to many different areas of life, including:

- Government, Education, Health and other public services
- Ecology, Sustainability and Regenerative Cultures
- Leading and Managing Organisations
- The Money System
- Psychotherapy and Arts and other Expressive Therapies
- Walking, Psychogeography and Mythogeography
- Movement and Somatics
- Innovation
- The Future and Future Studies

For books by Nora Bateson, Daniel Wahl, Russ Ackoff, Barry Oshry, John Seddon, Phil Smith, Bill Tate, Patricia Lustig, Sandra Reeve, Graham Leicester, Nelisha Wickremasinghe, Bill Sharpe, Alyson Hallett and other remarkable writers, please visit:

www.triarchypress.net

Lightning Source UK Ltd.
Milton Keynes UK
UKHW021446240121
377565UK00007B/94